Fo ‖‖‖‖‖‖‖‖‖‖‖‖‖‖‖‖‖‖‖‖‖
✔ KU-775-609

This book provides material for young people
to be introduced to the problems associated with
the misuse of drugs. It is intended to be a tool
for teachers, parents and health workers to use
as a starting point for conversations about the
many issues this topic throws up. It is non-
judgemental, offering informed choices.

This is by no means an exhaustive listing of every
particular drug a young person might be exposed
to, particularly the so-called 'hard drugs', but a
sounding board for discussion.

Aimed for use in conjunction with the author's
input, comprising a dynamic performance
followed by facilitation of informal workshops,
children work from the text in a relaxed
atmosphere, the emphasis on learning through
fun. For author availability, costs and sales,
contact:

The King's England Press
Education Liaison Department
Cambertown House, Commercial Road, Goldthorpe, Rotherham, S63 9BL
Tel/fax: 01484 663790
E-mail: fax4u@kingsengland.com

4

Beer Belly

My Dad has a beer belly
That hangs over his pants;
It often swings around
When he has a dance.

He claims he's an athlete,
Although he doesn't look it.
He doesn't drink beer by the glass
He drinks it by the bucket.

Fax 4 U

Did you know that a small glass of red wine, or half a pint of lager, contains around 90 calories and that a pint of beer has as many calories as 6 slices of bread but very little protein or vitamin? It's a case of "would my bum look big if I drank this?"

Why Shouldn't I?

All my friends do it,
Though it makes them choke;
My Mum and Dad do it,
So why shouldn't I smoke?

My favourite pop star does it
And he's a great bloke;
Some of my teachers do it,
So why shouldn't I smoke?

Why shouldn't I be a
Nicotine-stained, pea-brained,
Tar-craving, docker-saving,
Foul-smelling, teeth-yellowing,
Coughing and choking,
Tobacco smoking
Weak-willed joker?
Why shouldn't I be a smoker?

Fax 4 U

When people first start smoking it often makes them feel sick, dizzy and suffer headache. This is because tobacco contains tar, nicotine, carbon monoxide and other gases. So now you know what a car exhaust pipe feels like!

Sticky Situation

I once tried sniffing glue
Because I was bored, I suppose,
But it didn't work for me -
I just stuck my finger to my nose!

Fax 4 U

Glue is a solvent which is often sniffed or 'biffed' from a paper or plastic bag. It gives a user the sensation of drunkenness and some people pass out for a short while after sniffing it. This in itself can cause dangers, depending where the person is when using glue. Some come to a sticky end.

Sweet Goof!

In a cupboard I found a jar,
Full to the top with sweets.
I laughed to myself
"Have I found Mum's hidden treats?"

So I took a handful
Then started to eat
But they tasted bitter,
Not at all sweet.

When Mum found out
She went totally mad:
"Who put them in that jar?"
She screamed at my Dad.

She rushed me to hospital,
I asked, "Were they full of germs?"
She told me they were tablets
To rid the dog of worms!

Fax 4 U

Lots of prescription pills and medicines look like sweets or flavoured drinks. Just because they are medicines it does not mean that they are not dangerous. Leaving a medicine out of the box it came in, or eating something when you're not sure what it is, can be a big mistake.

Acting Like a Dope

My friend said he'd smoked a joint;
I thought him stupid, what was the point?
And how did he hold in his teeth
Such a big lump of beef?

Fax 4 U

A joint (or spliff) contains cannabis which is also known as wacky backy, dope (although this word now has a new meaning), skunk, hash, pot and many other names. There are lots of different views on cannabis but, remember, it is still a drug, whatever your view. Cannabis is an illegal drug but regarded as less harmful than most others by a lot of people. But, you might be spliffed off if *you* get caught smoking it!

Going Straight to the Head

I heard alcohol destroys brain cells,
I think it makes them rot.
That must leave you stupid -
Wow! My teacher must drink a lot!

Fax 4 U

If drunk in large measures over a long period, alcohol doesn't only affect your brain but also your liver and heart. In fact, if abused, it will affect your whole body. Binge drinking, when someone drink lots of alcohol all at once, can be just as dangerous. My Mum says, "Everything in moderation, except chocolate!"

Cough it Up

I drank a bottle of cough medicine,
It was made with lemon and honey;
I still have a bad cough
But it's made my head go funny.

Fax 4 U

Just because a medicine tastes nice it doesn't mean it's harmless. It may say honey and lemon in big letters on the bottle but, if you read the label, you'll find that it will contain other drugs as well. Taking too many over-the-counter medicines containing painkillers such as paracetamol and aspirin can be very dangerous. They are safe to use if you stick to the recommended dosage, so always read the label carefully. If you have a cough or cold, why not make yourself a warm honey and lemon drink, then you know that it's safe.

Money to Burn

Danny can't go bowling,
He says he's broke.
He bought some cigarettes
And watched his money go up in smoke.

Fax 4 U

Smoking can be an expensive habit. If you smoke twenty cigarettes a day costing £4.50 a packet (average price for 2003) it will cost you £1,638 a year. That's not to be coughed at!

The 'Hole' Truth

Aerosols caused a hole in the ozone
It is often said.
Well, my friend sniffs them
So he must have a hole in his head!

Fax 4 U

The propellant gases used in aerosols are what give the effect a user is after. Aerosols can affect your heart and cause heart failure if a user starts running around. Gases in aerosols and lighter fuel refills squirted directly into your mouth can freeze your airways and cause suffocation. But the good news is that they won't give you a hole in the head!

Staying Alive

I'm no one's mug,
I want to stay alive;
I'm only going to smoke and drink
Until I'm twenty-five.

Fax 4 U

Alcohol and tobacco are both addictive drugs, especially tobacco. Most people who drink don't have a problem with it but nearly all smokers find it hard to give up. To stop smoking you need a lot of will power, whoever he is!

Fax 4 U

Lots of people do things while drunk that they later regret; some are just harder to forget than others. So, if you ever wake up with a road map tattooed on your chest, make sure it has the way home marked on it for the next time you get so drunk!

Seeing the Whole Picture

Dad went with some friends
On a trip to Blackpool;
He came home blind drunk,
Acting like a stupid fool.

Next morning Mum was cross,
Dad said it was, "Just a bit of fun!"
But Mum wanted to know
Why he had a tattoo on his bum!

Keeping it in

Always read the label,
That's very good advice.
I once didn't
And boy, did I pay a price!

You see I had diarrhoea
But medical advice I didn't seek;
I just took a load of tablets
And I didn't pooh for a week!

Fax 4 U

If you take too many of some prescription drugs (overdose) you will have to go to hospital for a stomach pump which means all the contents of your stomach will be pumped out. So, if you don't want to see last night's curry again, stick to the recommended dosage.

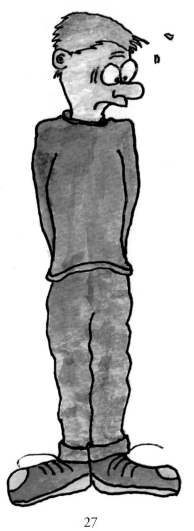

The Colour of Smoke

I often smoke
Cigarettes so mellow
But my teeth and fingers
Have now turned yellow.
It could be worse,
They could be green;
I think I'll smoke with my toes
And keep my fingers clean.

Fax 4 U

Not only does tobacco leave you with yellow teeth and fingers but it also makes your clothes smell and gives you bad breath. Snogging a smoker is like snogging an ashtray.

Making New Friends?

Before the school dance
We all went to the shops
And asked a man to buy us
A load of alcopops.

We drank them all,
I really felt great;
When I reached the dance
I was in a state.

It now makes me cringe,
Even after a week,
Because I kissed Barney Grimes
And he's the school geek!

Fax 4 U

Alcopops are very popular with younger drinkers because they don't taste like alcohol, which usually results in people becoming drunk more quickly. When you're drunk you feel as though you can say and do things you wouldn't dream of when sober. This can lead to all sorts of problems, some a lot worse than just snogging the school geek.

Mix 'n' Match

Dad took some tablets
All washed down with beer;
He now wishes he hadn't,
It's caused him to fear.

It isn't a danger
That cannot be seen
Because when he has a wee
It comes out green!

Fax 4 U

Using medicines with alcohol is dangerous as you are, in effect, taking two drugs at once. Alcohol can also affect the way that some prescription drugs work. And who wants green wee?

Solving the Situation

I don't know who the solvents are
Or from which country they come,
But these people are being picked on
So their lives can't be much fun.

Everyone is talking about them,
It's in the papers, on the news,
So lets all get together
And stop this solvent abuse.

Fax 4 U

Solvents are carbon-based compounds which can give the same effect as alcohol when breathed in. They can be found in many household items such as glue, paint, nail varnish remover, aerosols, petrol lighter fuels, cigarette lighter gas (butane) and lots more. Solvent users inhale the vapours through their nose or mouth and these vapours are absorbed through their lungs, rapidly reaching their brain to give a feeling of drunkenness. This is also known as glue sniffing, solvent abuse and volatile substance abuse (VSA). So now you know who solvents are and where they live - in your house!

Different Habits

I like to smoke,
My boyfriend likes sports;
You'll need a cigarette
If you see him in his shorts!

Fax 4 U

On the whole, less people are smoking in first world countries. However, this does not seem to be the case for teenagers and recent surveys suggest that smoking is increasing amongst young women. There must be a lot of lads walking around in shorts!

Straight Drinking

Proof, volume, units,
It's all a load of junk;
Everyone knows it's alcohol
That gets you really drunk.

Fax 4 U

Ready for a science lesson? Alcoholic drinks consist mainly of flavoured water and ethyl alcohol (ethanol). The term ABV means alcohol by volume, or how much water there is and how much alcohol. Are you with me so far? The unit of alcohol measure is used to determine medical guidelines for what are supposed to be safe drinking levels for men and women per week. Are you still there?

A unit of alcohol is equal to:

Half a pint of average strength beer
(approx 250 ml)

A regular glass (125 ml)
of weaker wine (9%)

A standard pub measure of spirits/
fortified wine such as sherry or port
(25 ml)

Those are the fax. I didn't say they
were interesting!

Who?

What kind of people take drugs?
Maybe they're evil type thugs?
Do doctors and teachers,
Vicars and shopkeepers
Drink them at home from mugs?

Fax 4 U

When thinking about people who use drugs it's easy to have an image of someone living rough, injecting themself with needles. But remember: anyone who smokes tobacco or drinks alcohol is taking drugs. And did you know that tea, coffee and soft drinks such as colas and even some chocolates contain something called caffeine which is a drug. It helps stimulate your body and combats tiredness, which is why people drink lots of coffee when they want to stay awake. I think I'd rather stay awake eating chocolate!

Side Effects

Gran says to alcohol, "No!
It makes the brain go slow."
Dad says "She's a bore,
It's not against the law.
She should try it and let herself go."

Mum and Dad go out once a week,
A dance and a singsong they seek.
They have a good laugh
And act really daft
Then Dad dances like a freak.

There was a man down our street,
His wife he would quite often beat.
It was the same every night,
He'd get drunk then pick a fight
So his wife left with a man called Pete.

There's a man who once sang in a band,
But these days he can hardly stand.
He now begs in the street
With an old hat at his feet
And a can of beer grasped in his hand.

Fax 4 U

There are many different views on alcohol ranging from "Don't touch it, it's evil!" to "I have to have a drink". Alcohol is a drug and to some people it is very addictive. Most people who drink alcohol just do so in moderation and have a good time. But alcohol can alter people's personality and some, usually men, become aggressive. It should be called the good the bad and the giggly.

A Tough One

Some drugs must be strong,
Others just a tub of lard
Because I've heard some are soft
While others are really hard.

Fax 4 U

Some people refer to drugs as "soft" or "hard" but this can be misleading. So-called soft drugs such as cannabis and LSD do not lead to physical dependence, the opposite of hard drugs which are generally believed to be much more dangerous. Using the terms "hard" and "soft" is a bit vague as even soft drugs can cause problems for users. Many drugs specialists will not use these terms for that reason. I wonder if alcohol is a soft drug? When my dad drinks beer he goes soft in the head!

Choices

"Should I drink this?
Should I 'use' that?"
Well, that's up to you,
But here are some facts.

Horrible Fax 4 U

About 110,000 people die prematurely in the UK each year through smoking-related diseases.

Between 70 to 100 young people in the UK die from solvent abuse each year.

Between 20,000 to 50,000 people each year in the UK are associated with alcohol. This includes deaths from alcohol-related accidents, cirrhosis of the liver and other diseases and death from overdose.

Those are the fax - the rest is up to you.

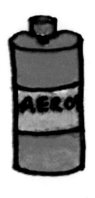

Other titles in the series
A6, colour, 48pp, £2.99

Bullying	**ISBN** 1 872438 87 3
Puberty	**ISBN** 1 872438 89 X
Relationships	**ISBN** 1 872438 88 1
Body Image	**ISBN** 1 872438 90 3

Making use of engaging material written by renowned children's comic poet Gez Walsh, the *Fax 4 U* series looks at the hazards of modern living facing today's young people. Each book uses the author's skilful use of humour to explore a particular topic and offer possible ways of dealing with the stress of growing up in the 21st century. Aimed for use in conjunction with the author's input (dynamic performance and informal workshops) pupils work from the texts and learn through fun in a relaxed atmosphere. Material is suitable for KS2 and Y7 of KS3.

The factual information in these books is based on a number of widely available public domain sources, including government sponsored publications, charities and other advisory bodies working in the areas covered.

While every effort has been made to ensure factual content is correct, neither the author nor the publisher can be liable for any matter arising from inaccuracy or any course of action followed as a result of reading these books. If you are concerned about any issues raised, seek advice from a qualified medical practitioner, teacher, health worker or parent.